NELL DUNN

Nell Dunn's plays include *Cancer Tales* (King's College, London, 2002, New Wolsey Theatre, 2005, and BBC Radio 4, 2009); *Babe* (2-Way Mirror Theatre Company, 1998); *Sisters* (Wolsey Theatre, Ipswich, 1994); *The Little Heroine* (Nuffield Theatre, Southampton, 1988); *Steaming* (Theatre Royal, Stratford East and the Comedy Theatre, West End; also produced in Norway, Sweden, Spain, Greece, Australia, New Zealand, Brazil and Hungary; winner of the SWET, Evening Standard and Susan Smith Blackburn Awards for the Best Play of 1981, revived at the Piccadilly Theatre in 1997); and *I Want* (Liverpool Playhouse, 1976).

Television includes *Every Breath You Take* (1985); and *Up the Junction* (1963), directed by Ken Loach.

Film includes *Poor Cow* (1966), directed by Ken Loach; and *Steaming* (1985), directed by Joseph Losey, with Vanessa Redgrave, Sarah Miles and Diana Dors.

Books include *My Silver Shoes, Grandmothers Talking to Nell Dunn, I Want* (with Adrian Henri), *Poor Cow, Up the Junction* (winner of the 1964 John Llewllyn Rhys Prize).

Other Titles in this Series

Nell Dunn

HOME DEATH

NICK HERN BOOKS
London
www.nickhernbooks.co.uk

A Nick Hern Book

Home Death first published in Great Britain as a paperback original in 2011 by Nick Hern Books Limited, 14 Larden Road, London W3 7ST

Home Death copyright © 2011 Nell Dunn

Nell Dunn has asserted her right to be identified as the author of this work

Cover image by iStockphoto.com/tepic
Cover design by Ned Hoste, 2H

Typeset by Nick Hern Books
Printed in Great Britain by CLE Print, St Ives, Cambridgeshire PE27 3LE

A CIP catalogue record for this book is available from the British Library

ISBN 978 1 84842 195 0

Home Death received a rehearsed reading at the Royal Academy of Dramatic Art, London, on 4 November 2010, and then at the Royal Society of Medicine, London, on 17 May 2011, as part of the Dying Matters Awareness Week. The cast was as follows:

LISA	Penelope Rawlins
MARY	Eleanor Rhodes
MICK	Edward Halsted
DIANA	Jane Maud
GEORGE	Edward de Souza
TREVOR	Keith Bartlett
LESLEY	Laura Fitzpatrick
NELL	Sara Kestelman
TRICIA	Jane Arden
JULIET	Laura Rees
JAMES	Robert Hickson
Director	Trevor Walker

The production was sponsored by Napp Pharmaceutical Holdings Limited and the National Council for Palliative Care.

The play's first fully staged production opened at the Finborough Theatre, London, on 10 July 2011, as part of Vibrant – A Festival of Finborough Playwrights, directed by Fiona Morrell.

The National Council for Palliative Care (NCPC) is the umbrella charity working to improve care for all who need it at the end of their lives. As part of its role NCPC leads the Dying Matters national coalition, which aims to support changing knowledge, attitudes and behaviours towards dying, death and bereavement and through this to make 'living and dying well' the norm.

NCPC is proud to be associated with *Home Death*, which highlights so many of the issues which often prevent people having their choices met at the end of life, as well as what makes dying well possible; often this starts simply by talking.
Information and help is available at Dying Matters, please visit **www.dyingmatters.org** or call **08000 214466**.

Napp Pharmaceutical Holdings Limited is committed to advancing the understanding and treatment of pain. Over the last 30 years, we have made available a wide range of innovative pain medicines to enhance the quality of patient care and expand the choice for healthcare professionals in treating different manifestations of short- and long-term pain.

We support those involved in delivering palliative care. We believe it is vital that people are given relief from pain and other symptoms, and that they and their families are provided with dedicated support. We also believe that people should be able to make informed choices about where they live and die, and the care that they receive.

We know that death and bereavement are challenging and complex issues, and we hope that by supporting *Home Death* we will help break down some of the barriers that may prevent people from receiving the care they would prefer. Further information on Napp can be found at **www.napp.co.uk**.

THE
NATIONAL
COUNCIL FOR
PALLIATIVE
CARE

This publication is supported by a grant from Napp Pharmaceutical Holdings Limited and the National Council for Palliative Care.

HOME DEATH

True Stories

Nell Dunn

In Memory of Dan Oestreicher

Foreword

Both my parents died at home. My sister and I knew little about death and they were not looked after as well as they might have been.

My partner died at home when I was alone with him and I knew little about how to comfort him.

I wanted to hear how other people had managed. I wanted to learn. I talked to people who had cared for a friend, mother, husband, wife who had died at home, and from these conversations I made *Home Death*.

Nell Dunn, 2011

Acknowledgements

Many people encouraged me during the writing of *Home Death*:

My friend and director Professor Trevor Walker, ever patient.
Eve Richardson, Sam Turner and Professor Mayur Lakhani
from the National Council for Palliative Care; Hilary Fisher
from Dying Matters; Clive Jones and Rachel Cummings from
NAPP; Professor Irene Higginson and Barbara Gomez da Silva
from King's College; Dr Ann McPherson, Ursula Daee, Clare
Moynihan and my ever kind and helpful agent, Sarah McNair,
and Judith Scott for her support. Thank you all.

And many generous people talked to me of their experience
including Margaret O'Brien, Leisha Fullick, Rupert Smith,
Juliet David, Diana Melly, Lesley Tutton, Trevor Walker and
Tricia Pank.

Characters

LISA
MARY
MICK
DIANA
GEORGE
TREVOR
LESLEY
NELL
TRICIA
JULIET
JAMES

This text went to press before the end of rehearsals and so may differ slightly from the play as performed.

One

MICK, LISA *and* MARY.

LISA. I am Lisa this is my sister Mary and this is Mick

Mick was one of my oldest friends   he met me and Mary when we were at university and he knew my mother very well

he never married, and I kind of hesitate to say this because Mary may not want to tell you all of this… I mean, the reality is that he was in love with her all his life, but she got together with somebody else

but still… and always… they used to meet twice a week   they went out together every single Friday night… every Friday night without fail they went to see a film… went for a meal

MARY. we were very close

LISA. he grew up in Hackney   he was a Classicist   he was a wonderful person

MARY. he was absolutely wonderful

LISA. he was small and dark and Jewish, extremely verbal   he was an enormous expert on films – particularly Westerns   he was an enormous expert on Classics

MICK. one morning I was teaching at Oxford and I became very unwell

LISA. and his students were so alarmed that they called for help, and the college tried to get him to go to the Radcliffe Hospital   and he absolutely refused

MICK. I'm not going there

LISA. they paid, which he was very triumphant about, for him to have a taxi that took him all the way to London – at God knows what expense – to the Royal Free Hospital because he was under a consultant there

MARY. but it seemed to me that the Royal Free was full of really mad people, and it wasn't restful

MICK. very sick people, very strange people – would shout at the nurses

Two

DIANA *and* GEORGE.

DIANA. I am Diana and this is George

I was down at our cottage near Newbury, and George was going for an ordinary check of his lungs and a scan because he'd had pneumonia   Candy, my daughter, went with him and they rang me up from the pub and Candy said, 'well, it's cancer'   and I was completely stunned   it was totally unexpected   if I'd expected it I would have gone with him

George came on the phone and he said

GEORGE. it's very small   I'll be fine   I don't want any treatment, and that's that

DIANA. I can't believe it   I thought it was me who was going to get cancer

for a while the cancer disappeared and then it came back   it was very slow

in the spring that year was the first time he didn't recognise me in the street   so the new cancer and the beginning of dementia happened at about the same time

so, that was the spring, and then, in December, I called in at Ronnie Scott's, where he was singing over Christmas

GEORGE *is singing.*

he isn't expecting me   and he didn't recognise me   he is sitting with Shirley, his secretary, and she said, 'George, your lady wants to talk to you'

and he looks up and he sees me, and he put out his hand to take mine, and kisses my hand, absolutely not recognising me

and Shirley says, 'George, it's Diana, your wife – look!'

I was laughing   but then I began to put two and two together and realise that he had dementia   and it was then that I rang the Admiral nurses   George's GP gave me their number

I got Madeleine and I told her what was happening   and she said, 'That is much more likely to be vascular dementia. With Alzheimer dementia it's a progression – a rather steady progression   but with vascular dementia, you can be fine one day and bad the next

we were going every three or four months for scans and each time the tumour had grown a little bit – three and a half centimetres, four centimetres…

I am quite got down by everything because he is incredibly forgetful   he loses all his bank cards and then he began to get aggressive – very aggressive to me and very aggressive to people in the street

he got a terrible thing about fat black women

'what about Bessie Smith?   she was a fat black woman, and you adore her   so, what is all this?'

I was very miserable   and then of course there is the lung cancer so, he had dementia and cancer   how long am I going to have to put up with this?

wouldn't it be better if he died?

he had a girlfriend to lunch – and Shirley was here – and he said

GEORGE. Shirley, I want you to do the washing up

DIANA. No, George   Shirley does not do the washing up   I'll do the washing up

GEORGE. I want Shirley to do the washing up

DIANA. George, Shirley is your secretary   you're a jazz singer and I don't expect you to mend the lights

GEORGE. I am not just a jazz singer   I'm a very, very important man

DIANA. this was just so unlike George, saying, 'I'm a very, very important man'

GEORGE. I am not staying in those hotels with the band any more   I am staying in a grand five-star hotel

Three

TREVOR *and* LESLEY.

TREVOR. I am Trevor and this is Lesley my sister

we lived in suburbia and when I was in my teens I was in a play at the Royal Court and then I wanted a different life   I was a rebel

my mum was upset about my leaving home and my sister, Lesley, felt she had to stay home – at least till she got married

LESLEY. my mother was very artistic

TREVOR. both our parents came from poor backgrounds   they both left school at fourteen   when I was born they were sleeping on friends' floors   they finally got a council house, but they were poor

tea was a piece of bread with sugar on it   it was years before I had a steak

our father did brilliantly and became a successful
businessman and manager of a company

LESLEY. Mum had been suffering from chronic diarrhoea and
nausea for about six weeks   she thought it was a tummy bug
and let it ride to see if she could sort it out herself   she had a
couple of trips to the doctor   I had to force her to go   she
wasn't really into doctors and medicine   and the third time
she went, the doctor decided she should go to hospital for
tests   the doctor asked her, 'does any of your family have a
history of bowel cancer?'

she was offended by that remark

TREVOR. it was the summer   I'd spent a bit of time with her
because I was teaching in Oxford, near where she lived   she
said that she hadn't been feeling well because she had an
upset stomach

she was very cross because the doctor had asked, 'was there
a history of bowel cancer in the family?'   and she felt very
angry that the doctor had said that completely out of the
blue, and it was very distressing, and why should he say that,
and of course there wasn't, and what a stupid thing to say

LESLEY. she collapsed in the supermarket   she rang me at
work at about five o'clock and she said, 'an ambulance is
coming and I am being admitted to hospital now'   I
thought, oh, my God, and rang my brother, Trevor, and I
rushed straight to Mum

TREVOR. Lesley phoned me up and said Mum had been
admitted to the local hospital and Lesley was unhappy about
this because she is a legal secretary and they had had a lot of
dealings with this hospital, and there was MRSA there, and a
lot of patients were suing for poor care   and that my mum
had gone into a ward and Lesley said it was filthy and there
were too many beds and only one or two nurses and she
couldn't get to the toilet because she was on a drip and she
could see blood spattered on the stand of the drip from the
previous patient   and so Lesley wanted to move her to a

private ward at the top of the hospital, and was that okay? and I said, 'yes, let's do that'

and when I arrived I was walking along this corridor and there was blood spattered all across the floor and it was disgusting   and then, suddenly, there was carpet and wood panels

LESLEY. I think she knew it was bad news   she started talking about my dad, who had died four years ago

on the Thursday she had another scan and a liver biopsy   and she went into this room and I had to wait outside   and Mum told me that when this process had finished the nurse said, 'is your daughter here?'   and Mum laughed and said, 'yes, she'll be waiting because she hasn't left my side since Monday'

I wasn't going anywhere but I was worried about my work   and I had made up my mind, stuff the job   I am going to see this through to the end   in fact, they were brilliant they gave me three weeks' compassionate leave on full pay   I told my boss what was happening, and he said, 'go, do whatever you need to do, and let us know'

I remember her lying in her bed, looking out of the window and saying to me, 'look at that tree, the colour...' she was very aware of beauty till the end

she wasn't worried about dying   the only time I ever saw her cry was when we were in the hospital and she is in the middle of some tests and we are waiting to have a scan and she is sitting in a wheelchair and I am sitting with her and this woman went by on a trolley, shouting and delirious, and Mum said, 'that's not going to happen to me, is it?   please don't let that ever be me'   and she broke down and cried and I said, 'Mum, that won't ever be you, ever, ever'

Four

DAN *and* NELL.

NELL. I am Nell and Dan was my lover

Dan caught a ferocious bronchitis, had a chest X-ray, and a six-centimetre tumour was found on his lung   he was operated on, recovered and came home to his flat over the road from me and with wonderful treatment on the NHS was well for five years

and then it came back and he had more treatment, got well again, and then suddenly was extremely ill and taken into hospital and hated it and the general consensus was he is going to die any moment and he should go home

so too weak to look after himself he came to my house... my lover for thirty-five years but separate houses... I am a writer and can only work in an empty house... was suddenly being carried up the stairs in a chair by two paramedics and although that same morning a horrible hospital bed had been delivered and his chair was heading towards it he pointed majestically to my bed and said 'there!'   and that's where for eighteen months he slept and that's where he died

Five

TRICIA *and* PHILIP.

TRICIA. I am Tricia and Philip is my husband

Philip's diagnosis was badly handled   he had appendicitis and was rushed into hospital and that was taken out   the houseman said to him, 'when you recover we want you to have a barium enema because we aren't entirely happy about your gut'

so, six weeks later, Philip went to have this, and we were sitting in outpatients for ages and ages, and finally we were ushered into the room and the surgeon, whom I knew because I'd worked with him when I was nursing, came in   he just stood in the door and said, 'well, I suppose you've realised what the result of your X-ray is?'

he was vile   he said, 'I'll need to do some surgery'

I said, 'I want a second opinion'   I didn't want him to operate I'd worked with him and didn't like him   'I want the notes and the X-rays'   he wasn't very pleased

we went to another NHS surgeon   he was refined and ethical and brilliant at his job, and he did the operation

then we knew the cancer was in the liver   the tumour had caused the original blockage in the appendix

Six

TREVOR *and* LESLEY.

TREVOR. and my mum was in this small room with her own bathroom, and she was much happier because she could get to the loo, and Lesley was there

it was nice but it was £550 a night, and that was not including medical care   Lesley was angry because the doctor said he was off to a conference in London for two days and he wouldn't be able to examine Mum till he got back, or talk to her

LESLEY. 'but that's £1,100 just because this guy is going to a conference'

TREVOR. nobody came, so Lesley and I went down to the canteen to have lunch   there is something about hospital canteens – institutional, unwelcoming and horrible   then we went back up and a young doctor was in there talking to her he was saying there is an abnormality in the tests, but he didn't explain and in the end she said, 'have I got cancer?'   and he said, 'yes   and she said, 'how long have I got to live?'   and he said, 'these things can be quick' so, I took him outside and I tried to make it easy for him to tell me and he said again, 'it can be quick…'   but he wouldn't look at me, he looked down… and then he said, 'probably, six months'

LESLEY. Trevor came down for the appointment with the consultant on Friday he told her, 'you've got cancer of the bowel'   and she said, 'how long have I got?' – just like that

the doctor said she could have treatment but he couldn't be sure it would buy her more time   and she said, 'well, I've just got to get on with it'

Trevor and I were finding it very hard not to cry   we didn't want to cry in front of her   she wouldn't have liked that   but I broke down and she said, 'now, come on'   she wanted to be on her own for a bit, which I thought was right for her   so, Trevor and I went outside the door and we were hugging and crying

then we went back in and she said, 'I don't want treatment so don't even think about it, and I want to go home and be in my own room in my own bed'

Seven

MICK, LISA *and* MARY.

LISA. and there were all sorts of complications because Mick had a GP in Oxford and in order to get any access, any services in Hackney, he had to have a GP in Hackney   and it's impossible to get a GP in Hackney   and there was this kind of health centre which was the only place that was going to take him, where the flotsam and jetsam of the world fetched up, there were all these babies and refugees, and hardly anyone spoke a word of English, including the doctors   and it was an amazing place

MICK. I can't go there   I don't want to go there

MARY. Mick had a flat in Stoke Newington   it was pretty, small and very light and he'd only recently moved in there he lived on his own

MICK. I am diagnosed with liver cancer   it is inoperable   and I decide not to have any treatment   I decide that I'm not going to be a sick person

MARY. I was there when the specialist gave him the news   it was very hard but it was obvious he was dying   he was in a pretty bad way

MICK. I want to die at home

LISA. but first he goes to Rome with Mary

MICK. I love Rome   I love Italy   and I spend thousands of
    pounds   I buy paintings   I buy rugs

MARY. he buys an Armani suit

LISA. the minute Mick is diagnosed I need to get him booked
    into a hospice   and this needs to happen, and that needs to
    happen   and he absolutely refuses to engage with any of
    that   the only thing he is worried about...

MICK. where am I going to be buried?

LISA. he didn't want to be cremated

MICK. I want to be buried in London

MARY. he's an absolute Londoner, through and through

    and all London cemeteries are full up

LISA. so I got him one of the last graves in Highgate
    Cemetery   that was the only thing that interested him

MICK. getting my grave

Eight

DIANA *and* GEORGE.

DIANA. he is still going out and about a bit on his own and
    nearly always in a taxi   he went on the Tube to a party at
    the Whitechapel Gallery so all he had to do was get on the
    Tube at the end of the road, which I took him to by car, and
    he had to get out at Aldgate   he got there okay, but he got
    hopelessly lost coming back, and so I realise I must never
    again let him go on the Tube alone

and then in the January it all got much worse and I began to be very worried about him going away to sing because there was no way he could stay in a strange hotel   and the band were in complete denial about his dementia because, once he was on the stage, he would remember his words

GEORGE *is singing.*

the band wanting him to go on singing   and he wanted to go on singing   and I wanted him to go on singing

he was a performer

GEORGE *is singing.*

there were many visits to the hospital   he had lots of different things wrong with him as well as the lung cancer   psoriasis   he had stomach ulcers   he had a heart condition   feet...

this woman was doing his feet and she was doing his feet and he was just incredible about me   dreadful!

GEORGE. she's this, she's that   'she doesn't respect me'

DIANA. 'George, I'm in the room'   I was in and out doing things and he didn't care

GEORGE. 'she never says she loves me'

DIANA. 'what am I doing all day except taking care of you?   I am making it possible for you to sing   I drag you up to do a gig and stay in a dog-friendly hotel so I can go with you...'

I spend ages in the supermarkets looking for food that would tempt you because you are very difficult to feed   no appetite   and one week you only wanted smoked salmon, and then

GEORGE. 'why do you always get me smoked salmon?   all you ever get me'

DIANA. and then he would want a one-egg omelette, which I used to find very hard to make   a one-egg boiled egg, yes, but a one-egg omelette is difficult but I enjoyed some of that

I like taking care of people because you've got care and control if you are doing the caring   so I liked choosing him biscuits that he might like – he had a terrifically sweet tooth

GEORGE. 'I want you to make me that nice pudding with jam that you used to make when I was a little boy'

DIANA. 'but George, I don't think that was me'

well, I do know how to make rice puddings with a dollop of jam on it   that's fine

then I used to buy him really disgusting sweets – Black Forest gateau, and he ate them

Nine

TREVOR *and* LESLEY.

LESLEY. when things first started and Mum was admitted to hospital, Trevor was in London and I was living down the road   it was important that I was the organiser, and Trevor was happy with that

TREVOR. I said, 'are you frightened?'   and she said, 'no, our dad took it on the chin and so will I'   it was a working-class approach   she'd lived through the war

LESLEY. I always knew she wanted to die at home because she had made a living will years ago   it was very important to her that she had no treatment   she had seen a lot of friends who had gone down that road and she felt if her time had come, so be it

because she had moved from NHS to private, although it was in the same hospital, she couldn't get an ambulance to take her home she said, 'I want to go home now'   so I took her in my car

Ten

DIANA *and* GEORGE.

DIANA. and I think I used to get through the nights of worry by thinking how will I arrange the house when things get worse   we took it for granted that he would stay at home

I was getting a lot of support from Admiral nurses – I was discussing it with them   at that moment George's bedroom was on the second floor and his sitting room was on the first floor, and my room and the kitchen were on the ground floor   so I would think to myself, okay, I could move him down to the first floor but there's no toilet on that level   so what would I do?   I could put in a stairlift   there's a little kitchen   I could get rid of that and put a little toilet and shower in there, next to the sitting room, and he could sleep there

I could spend all night thinking about the way I would organise the house for when he got really ill   because at that time I had no idea if it would be weeks, months – or years, even   goodness knows how long it was going to be   or what state he would be in

would it, on the other hand, be better to move him down to the ground floor?   but then there was the smoking problem   by this time he was smoking very heavily again   and I certainly didn't try to stop him   but I'm asthmatic   and as the kitchen was downstairs I thought, well, I can't have him downstairs and me getting bad-tempered because I'm breathing in all his smoke   and then I thought, well, maybe I'll move him down to the commode situation   there'll be a bed in his sitting room and there'll be a commode so that would solve that one   I never really made any firm decisions I just would think, well, if that happens we'll have plan A, and if that happens then we'll have plan B

that's how I relieve my anxiety   I'll sort out the problem before it happens   and in some way that's a sign of a pessimist because I'm obviously thinking of the worst situation   what I never thought about was he'd be in hospital and I'd have to visit   that absolutely never entered my thoughts

Eleven

DAN *and* NELL.

NELL. Dan wanted to die at home   he was on twenty-four-hour oxygen   nothing more could be done for him   however, the few days predicted on his discharge from hospital became eighteen months of good life

the week before he died, he asked me to sit with him   he wanted to tell me something   Primrose, our dog, was on his lap   I sat on the sofa across from his chair, and he told me

'I know I am going to die soon and I am ready for it   I want to die well   but I don't quite know how to get from here to there'

he went on speaking but I was deaf   I said nothing to reassure him nothing about the huge love I felt for him   nothing about the happiness he had brought me   nothing about what a wonderful lover he was

I sat, frozen in silence, while Dan and Primrose looked at me   I didn't believe he was going to die   I knew he was but I didn't believe it

eventually, he said, 'thank you for listening to me'   I got up and silently left the room, dizzy with shock and terror

later, I said, 'don't worry if you pee and poo on the floor   it
is a wooden floor, I can easily wipe it up'   I knew he
worried when he got up in the night

'that is so reassuring, my love,' he said

the next day was my birthday and he sent me to the Conran
shop to buy myself a present... 'you wanted an overnight
bag, go and choose one... take my card'   when I came back
he examined the bag with great care   'I think it's very well
made,' he said

he was in charge of his own medicines but towards the end
he wanted me to do them for him   I made a list and took
them over to the bed and he made a little dent in the duvet
and I put them in and he took them, one by one, swallowing
them down with water

these moments were precious   you wouldn't think so, but
they were

he got a sore on his bottom   the district nurse put a plaster
on it but soon after she left, it fell off   'can you put another
one on for me?' he asked

'I'm not your wife,' I said   'oh, all right, I will'   and I did,
and it was fine

and later still he said, 'my love, you are so kind to me'

I am shocked at some of the things I said: 'I can't wash your
feet today, I haven't time'

'no, you can't have a stairlift because it would spoil the
carpet...' spoil the carpet, spoil the carpet

I was so angry   he was going to leave me   he was going to
abandon me

he was going to die

and, quite simply, I couldn't bear it

Twelve

DIANA *and* GEORGE.

DIANA. and then there was one day when we saw his oncologist and I said, 'what's the prognosis?'   and this would have been in November

I didn't mean when is he going to die?   I meant what happens now?   but apparently it means when am I going to die?   and so the doctor said, 'well, George, you'll see this Christmas, but you won't see the next one'

but George doesn't hear properly

GEORGE. 'what did he say?'

DIANA. you'll see this Christmas but perhaps not next

GEORGE. 'well, I don't like Christmas, anyway'

DIANA. and I think I felt better for knowing

I told George I hadn't known what prognosis meant

GEORGE. 'well, that's very ignorant of you'

Thirteen

TREVOR *and* LESLEY.

LESLEY. I whizz home and change her sheets, hoover her room, and make it nice and comfortable and put a lamp on   it was early evening and it looked really comfortable and nice

I put a hot-water bottle in her bed

then I fetch her

we get home   she is very weak   she can't get up the
stairs   they were steep stairs in her little house   I couldn't
lift her, or hold her even, because you couldn't have two
people, side by side on the stairs, too narrow

so, she went up on her hands and knees   I went up behind her

when she walked into the bedroom, she went, 'oh, that looks
so nice. I am home at last'

I helped her off with her clothes... then she just fell into bed
and lay back and nodded off, and looked content   really
happy

TREVOR. after my dad died she was lonely   she wasn't really
complete without him   it was an old-fashioned kind of
marriage that lasts for ever

when Mum knew she was going to die she wanted to get on
with it, so she mostly stopped eating and drinking and she
probably hastened her death   she was someone who just got
on with things

she had to die, so let's get on with it

by now she had a morphine driver

I said to the nurse, 'you know what our mother wants and
you know what we want'   she was a kind of midwife to
help the dying

LESLEY. she wasn't in pain   they had given her an anti-nausea
drug so she wasn't running to the loo all the time   she said,
'I would sooner be in pain than have the nausea'   she
wanted to be on her own.

I was given a letter to give to her GP   so, I settled her into
bed and then took this letter about five or six o'clock   I
walked into the surgery and it must have been the end of the

day because it was deserted and I remember this almighty feeling of loneliness   that I had brought this woman home, who was dying, and I don't know what to do

I don't know what to do   she doesn't want any help   she doesn't want any medication   and I am scared   Trevor would have been there if I'd asked him to be   I remember saying to the receptionist, 'I've got to hand this in to you, but I don't know what to do'   so lonely and panicky   'I've got my mum at home, and she's dying' and I started crying   and she said, 'don't worry, there is help'   and she told me about district nurses and community nurses   'and if you are worried about the night, there is the Marie Curie nurses who will come and sit with your mum all through the night and help her'   thank goodness there is help   and from there I organised everything

TREVOR. watching my mother die was somehow connected to my children being born   it was beyond everyday superficiality   it was very real and I was in touch with something that goes back thousands of years   it was very comforting

LESLEY. for the next few days Mum was eating a little bit and sitting up in her bed, and she said, 'you know, it's not that bad having cancer, because lots of people have it and they go on for ages   I can just potter around Charlbury and stay at home, and I'll be all right'   that went on for two or three days, and then on the Tuesday she didn't want to get up or eat   it was then I decided she needed help

I got hold of the doctor and said, 'could you get a district nurse to come over?'

they were absolutely brilliant   in those five or six days leading up to her death they became my best friends   they were amazing   like my mother was the only patient they ever had

Fourteen

MICK, LISA *and* MARY.

LISA. Mick thought he would like to be at home, sick for a
    while, and he just assumed that Mary would look after him

    I did have one meeting with the people at the Royal Free and
    they were obsessed by the bed   he couldn't go home unless
    there was a proper hospital bed

MARY. and they did not have a bed   there was a team of people
    that I was supposed to meet about the end of life, that was sup-
    posed to liaise with the Hackney Social Services, and there
    were problems with that as well   and in the end Mick just got
    his own way and they let him out of hospital without the bed

MICK. I got a cat, cos I thought, well, I'm going to be home,
    sick for a while... I'd like a cat

MARY. and so he purchased this incredibly expensive, young,
    pedigree cat

LISA. and he had this kind of grand idea that food would be
    brought in from restaurants and his friends would be in
    attendance   and that it would be okay

    Mary and I met him at the flat   but nothing was really set up
    to look after him

MICK. I went up in the lift in a wheelchair   I had this little
    bedroom that was up a flight of stairs   I couldn't go up them
    and I had this tiny little pine bed that I'd had from when I
    was a child at home   and it was in the middle of the living
    room   that's where I wanted to be

LISA. so, he arrived and I think the cat arrived at about the
    same time

MARY. and the kitten was traumatised   it was a very traumatic
    time for the kitten as well   and Mick couldn't really take the

kitten in   they didn't really bond   the kitten was running around, kind of agitated, and started peeing in the sink out of agitation

LISA. we made up the bed and he was very, very poorly   and the next morning he was in a terrible state and Mary and I didn't know what to do   and he screamed at us

MICK. 'oh, leave it alone   leave it alone'

LISA. but he needed something

MARY. Social Services were meant to be delivering a special bed and special handrails   and they delivered a vast amount of support materials – and just kind of dumped them

LISA. a large number of aids arrived in the flat: bathing chairs, commodes

the bed never arrived

MARY. Mick was obsessed with having showers, so I helped him with that but he didn't need all the paraphernalia that they delivered   it was in the way, and the bed itself never arrived

LISA. he is a pedigree cat   he is a beautiful mackerel-coloured fluffy young cat

MARY. well, he was lovely, but he was also a bit of a nuisance   it was quite a hectic time   a lot of kerfuffle

we kind of cared for him between us   Jessica, his student, was there a lot   Lisa was there a lot   I was there a lot

LISA. towards the end they provide this service when somebody sits up with you all night   and I was very keen to have this service because, well, because we needed it, because Mary and I were going to and fro from full-time work

MARY. I think the worst thing for me was that I needed back-up because I felt scared and hopeless

that was the awful thing   I didn't know what to do   I didn't know how to help him

Fifteen

DAN *and* NELL.

NELL. three days before he died he was visited by the hospice
    nurse, who knelt down beside the bed – our double
    bed   Dan never slept in the horrible, scary, cold hospital bed
    that sat unused, cluttering up our bedroom for a year and a
    half   anyway, the nice hospice nurse knelt down, perhaps to
    be on the same level with his patient while they discussed his
    discomforts   he was a nice man and he reassured Dan:
    'your care will be every bit as good as if you were in the
    hospice   you will have hospice at home'   and he sent a fax
    to the GP for a morphine prescription

    later that day the district nurse came with a plastic box,
    which contained a morphine driver, and it was left in the
    bedroom   this was Thursday

Sixteen

TRICIA *and* PHILIP.

TRICIA. I had to tell Philip's mother that he had cancer   her
    daughter had died three years earlier   I didn't beat about the
    bush   I told her exactly what it was and what was
    happening   it was cruel   it is unnatural to lose both your
    grown-up children

    when Philip was struggling up to the hospital for his
    chemotherapy, it was a wonderful nurse who said, 'I think you
    need some palliative care for the pain'   and she fixed it all up
    he had a low dose of chemo till we went to Greece, and it
    was clear it wasn't having any effect

we had a very physical relationship, and sometimes you
don't need words   we had a very telepathic relationship, and
sometimes you can just hug and you know what is going on,
which makes it much easier   I think we knew what each
other was thinking

the talking was important – with his mother and with the
children

and for every day of Philip's last six months everybody was
so close

that's one of the things about dying of cancer: time

people have this strange vision sometimes of protecting
people through lying   it never works   you only protect
people with the truth

Seventeen

DIANA *and* GEORGE.

DIANA. we were beginning to be able to have a bit of a joke
    about things in a way, and things were definitely getting a bit
    easier   I'm not quite sure why   maybe because I saw there
    was an end in sight

    and he is getting much more frail, losing his appetite, staying
    in bed most of the time, waking up to have a cigarette

    the doctor said, 'I will put you in touch with the Macmillan
    nurses' and I remember that cold hand on my heart   I
    thought, once you get Macmillan nurses the end is in sight

Eighteen

TREVOR *and* LESLEY.

LESLEY. we had one woman in to wash her, another to check
   her bedding and help her on and off the commode   then
   there was another woman coming in in the late afternoon to
   wash her face and help her do her teeth and hair

   the doctor and the district nurse worked together over the
   medicines

   we went from nothing to everything   people were so
   good   I was overwhelmed

Nineteen

MICK, LISA *and* MARY.

LISA. and the Social Services were awful   they didn't appear
   to be very well trained for the job in hand   and they sent in
   a supply of people overnight   I thought it would be a nurse
   but it was a different person every night – who just sat
   there   that home care was awful

   Jessica had just graduated   she was one of his Classics
   students   and she moved in   she moved in and stayed with
   him   she was young but she was strong

   so she slept in the bed upstairs

MARY. and we put Mick to bed in the little pine bed… and
   that's where he slept…

LISA. he got up to pee

MARY. and I gave him a shower

LISA. the district nurse came in and out – but we needed someone to take command and say, 'this is what you do'

MARY. and 'this is when we're coming'

LISA. and 'this is when we're going'

MARY. and 'this is how we plump up his pillows'

LISA. or 'this is how we help him get to the loo'

what they were interested in was administering drugs and writing in the notebook that they'd been   that's all they were concerned about

MARY. and I don't think they related to Mick as a person

LISA. all these different people came

MICK. I had to explain to them all what was going on   and so there wasn't anybody to build a relationship with… make friends with…

MARY. and he was really patient, and he was explaining to them about his condition, what he wanted, what the situation was

LISA. and then they'd disappear and another one would come, and he'd do it all again

MICK. I am absolutely determined not to have morphine

All exit.

JULIET *and* JAMES *enter – they are carrying coffee and muffins, they sit and talk to each other, face to face: sometimes one may say to the other on an improvised level – 'tell me more,' etc., to show they are talking to each other.*

Twenty

JULIET *and* ROLLIE.

JULIET. I am Juliet   I'd known Rollie since I was a baby

Rollie was a fostered child – fostered here at the farm by my grandparents in the sixties – and, when my father was young, very close to Dad   very close…

Rollie had lung cancer and he was in the hospital but there was nothing more they could do for him   so Dad said, 'go down to the hospital and pick him up and bring him here'

so I went and picked him up in the car   he came up to the farm, which is a wild place up in the hills   he went into the flat at the back of the house and the district nurse came every day

he was a bit of a drunkard

he loved playing wild games   he once streaked at a cricket match   the police knew him

Twenty-One

JAMES *and* OLIVIA.

JAMES. I am James   Olivia is my wife

we hadn't been married long   she was American

we were having quite a tricky time, a lot to do with her being away from America, and she was having thoughts about what she was doing in England… she hadn't set out to have a job so she had time to doubt her existence over here, and that was causing problems with us

eight years ago she had been diagnosed with non-Hodgkin's lymphoma   she was being topped up with something I thought was a routine top-up   it never caused her any discomfort

then – I can't remember what the technical term is – it changed from dormant to active, and at that point she had chemotherapy over a period of four months, until the beginning of September so, from April to September she is going in and out of hospital, having things done

the children, my stepchildren – Jason is thirteen and Rose is ten – are at home with us in Winchester, in our rented house   they went to school nearby

we live a normal family life   I am training to be a teacher so I got leave and am able to devote myself to Olivia and the family   so, there wasn't too much strain here   there was enough time to do everything, and that was fine

it was a matter of doing the chemotherapy   it was a matter of what the doctor said at the end of each bout, and it was always, 'it hasn't really done the job, we'll try something else'   and then, 'it hasn't really done the job, we'll try something else'   three times in a row 'it hasn't really done the job, we'll try something else' then it was September, and he said, 'we've done all we can'

they gave her radiotherapy but even then they said it was a very long shot   we never ever talked about her dying   to the very last minute she was always hoping that she wouldn't   so we never had that conversation

oddly, our relationship was probably the best it ever was   it makes you strip away all the nonsense it was sort of the purest and most simple   we just love one another and there is none of that domestic crap that gets in the way of a relationship   it is a bizarrely happy period... a very, very happy period because I could just love her without any of the peripheral stuff

it was something you could never guess... people who haven't been through it, I don't think can quite understand   and being in the position of a carer is extraordinarily fulfilling   you never doubt what you are doing, like you do in your normal life

one night Olivia got into problems   she faints from pain when she is on the loo   it's something to do with inside and I call an ambulance, which is something of an overreaction, but she conks out completely   she passes out through pain, and I ring a local parent: 'can you take the children?'   it's the middle of the night

so the ambulance came and I am able to go with her

Twenty-Two

JULIET *and* ROLLIE.

JULIET. well, we are having supper in the kitchen and Rollie was a laugh that night... talking about his life... all the wild things he had got up to... then he says, 'you girls can go home because your dad and I have things to talk about'

he wanted Dad to himself   Dad had been his fellow
conspirator when they were teenagers   the two of them had
got up to all kinds of wickedness and I think Rollie wanted to
go back there with Dad to talk about all the fun they had had

his voice was weak and I knew he had just wanted to be with
Dad   he loved Dad and Dad loved Rollie   he had been
happy here as a kid   it was a wonderful place to grow
up   it was a place to feel free

Twenty-Three

JAMES *and* OLIVIA.

JAMES. the GP came around a lot, and it was about pain
    management by now   we get a wheelchair… it's a lovely
    Indian summer and I wheel her around Winchester, so she
    isn't bedridden   she got weaker quite quickly   then she
    wants a party because she suddenly feels better   she didn't
    feel sick

    friends from America came over   I book them into bed and
    breakfasts   so there is a lot to do   I am cooking for every-
    body and there are the children   almost a party   it's fun for
    her   she never gnashed her teeth about what's happening to
    her

    the doctor found us a full-time helper: Jenny   she's
    wonderful   she was one of the nurses at the hospital, and we
    managed to get her privately

    Jenny is the centre of everything   she made it into a calm
    experience   if she hadn't been the way she was… she is
    wonderful

    I go off to Ireland because Olivia reads somewhere that there
    is a doctor who makes some potion out of bougainvillea   so

I go to Ireland to get this stuff, and I bring it back, a sort of capsule   she thinks it will be a miracle   suddenly she will be cured   but nothing...

Twenty-Four

JULIET *and* ROLLIE.

JULIET. suddenly, the next morning, Dad comes running into the kitchen in a great state   Rollie's lung had burst and the pain was excruciating, and Dad didn't know what to do   Rollie is roaring in pain

the doctor comes and says, 'you have to understand: as soon as the injection is given he won't come back   I don't know how long he'll last   it could be as long as a week, but he won't come back'

Twenty-Five

JAMES *and* OLIVIA.

JAMES. she tells the children, 'I'm ill but I'm going to get better'   then she gets worse   'it'll be okay'

then... 'I may not get better'

I don't say goodbye to her because somehow you can't say goodbye – you're always hoping, and she's always hoping   I suppose other people do but certainly with us there was always this hope that it would be all right in the end

the last really sensible conversation I had with her was about the fact I'd taken a part-time job in the local school and

within the first week of my work there I'd been offered a
full-time job, which is what I'd been trying to get the whole
time I was with her   so it was very good news for me   she
said, 'oh, I love you!'   and I joked that she only loved me
because I'd now got a full-time job, because I'd been slightly
under-employed most of my time with her   and she said, 'I
love you anyway   I love you'

we move her downstairs to what was my study and the
hospital sent a fancy bed that moved up and down   she
can't manage the stairs any more   and her first husband,
Den, came over, which wasn't a bad thing except he did get
pissed in our house   so that was quite weird

I was cooking my basic shepherd's-pie-and-peas thing   but
he is an excellent cook   so he would cook us something
delicious and get pissed at the same time   his routine is
getting pissed in the early evening, while cooking   and then
it was her and me, like being a sort of mummy and daddy
and the three children, and him being incoherently drunk
while trying to serve out the food

Olivia is very weak by now   Jason wanted to go to summer
camp, and his father and I sat him down and said, 'it's a
possibility that Mummy may die'   and he said, 'I want to
go'   he was finding it very difficult

Rose was ten   she wants to stay home with Mummy   the
doctor took me and Den aside and said, 'do you want me to
crank up the morphine?'

and Den said, 'why would you want to crank up the
morphine?' she isn't in pain   she is still awake some of the
time

she was alive   she was a person   we would have been
killing her, even if she did die three days later   so I said,
'no'   but she is conscious less and less

Jenny was there, holding everything together

Twenty-Six

JULIET *and* ROLLIE.

JULIET. all I knew was we needed to stop the pain

Rollie was in agony, his body all tense   not speaking *roaring*!

we get him into bed   the doctor said to me, 'can you deal with a dead body?'   'why are you asking?   of course I can deal with a dead body'

I thought I don't care what happens   you've got to get him out of his huge pain

he might die that night, and he wanted to know if I can cope with having a dead body in the house

what are you talking about?   of course I can

I was shocked that he would ask that question   and he said, 'you have no idea what people are like   they will not have a dead body in the house, even if it is their closest relative   they want it gone immediately'

I really don't have a problem with a dead body in the house   so, the doctor said, 'okay, I needed to know'   I think he didn't want me ringing up in the middle of the night saying, there's a dead body here and you've got to deal with it

what's the problem with a dead body?   somebody shrieking in agony: yes. I have a problem with that

we had already rung Rollie's daughter and told her he had had this injection

he is going to die   he's had an injection, and he's sleeping

Twenty-Seven

JAMES *and* OLIVIA.

JAMES. then… it's extraordinary   I watch her die   she did this sort of little rattle in her throat, and then she dies… gently dies… very gently…

I don't do much crying   I have a quick blub   Den closes her eyes and her mouth   I sit with her for a while

Rose comes back from school, and I tell her, 'Mummy has died   would you like to see her?'   and she said, 'yes' and she came in and said, 'is she really dead?'   and she wiggled her big toe

Twenty-Eight

JULIET *and* ROLLIE.

JULIET. his daughter comes, and I am there, and Dad is there

we leave her alone with him, and she lights candles and sits with him for about an hour and a half

she calls me and says, 'I think he may be going'   so I went in and the two of us sit there together

suddenly he stops breathing   it was calm

it wasn't horrible at all and he goes – very peacefully

it was a good death, once he had had the injection

JULIET *and* JAMES *exit*.

Twenty-Nine

DIANA *and* GEORGE.

GEORGE *is singing*.

DIANA. there was a gig in Barnes, and we got him there in his wheelchair and he was lifted onto the stage in his wheelchair, and then of course all the audience would shout and clap at anything   and all the band saying there's nothing wrong with him because he gets a standing ovation, because they're clapping him in a wheelchair, and he's managing to sing

and then there was a day when all the children and all the grandchildren came over to see him and he said he didn't think he could get down the stairs   so, they were making a film about George's end of life, the dementia and everything   so, the cameraman and sound man carried him down in his wheelchair, down the stairs and into the garden

it was the beginning of June, and it was lovely, and we all sat there and he sat with Tom, our son, and was very particular about what he wanted done at his funeral   and he made a list of what he was going to wear

GEORGE. I am going to have spats on my feet and a bowler hat

DIANA. and I suddenly realised he was dressing himself like a Magritte

GEORGE. and I'm going to be sitting in the front pew, watching

DIANA. no, George   you're not going to be sitting in the front pew

you are going to be in the coffin

GEORGE. oh, yes. I forgot about that

Thirty

MICK, LISA *and* MARY.

MICK. I grow weaker and weaker   difficult to walk   difficult
to breathe

LISA. he coughed up blood in the middle of the night

MICK. I got Mary up in the middle of the night and coughed up
blood

MARY. I was there

LISA. or, he may have been on his own   I'm not too sure

MARY. I was there

LISA. there was blood everywhere, and Mary had to deal with
that

MICK. I was determined not to have morphine   I was
determined to remain conscious and go on living

I want nice bedlinen and pyjamas

LISA. and we got in a taxi and went to Liberty's and we bought
him this fantastic bedding and this wonderfully feathery
blanket

MICK. this blanket was like angora, and it was knitted and it
was mauve and fluffy

MARY. and we bought that, and we bought these pillows that
cost hundreds of pounds

MICK. they were, you know, just so comfortable

LISA. and we bought this beautiful mauve bedding   we spent
hundreds and hundreds of pounds: I spent about seven
hundred quid

MICK. no   I paid for it in the end   I paid you back!

LISA. did you?

and we got fabulous linen pyjamas, that Mary's still got

MICK. linen pyjamas, that cost a fortune

MARY. pure linen pyjamas   I bought those   and we bought all this lovely stuff, and that afternoon   he was in a bad way – very, very poorly

MICK. I couldn't get comfortable   I couldn't breathe

Thirty-One

TREVOR *and* LESLEY.

TREVOR. I remember being on either side of the bed, with Lesley and my mother holding both our hands and saying, 'my special ones'

LESLEY. she was lying in bed, and she looked lovely   and Trevor and I were each side of the bed, holding her hands, sitting on the floor   and she looked at us, from one to the other, and she said, 'my favourite two'

I'll never forget that

Thirty-Two

MICK, LISA *and* MARY.

LISA. the next day was the Sunday, and on the Sunday night I spent the night with him   and that was the bad, bad night   that was the bad night   Mary had spent the day with him, and I got there Sunday evening, and I sat up all night with him

Mick was conscious all night, and this sitter came – this Jamaican woman   and Jessica was there as well   and so there were three people with him that night, and it was the most horrible night, and he was screaming in pain   this Jamaican woman was completely useless   she sat on the settee

she got up every now and then to write in this bloody notebook

she didn't do anything   she didn't say anything   she just sat there   and so Jessica and I tried to calm him, but Mick was screaming in agony

MICK. am I dying?

LISA. I don't know   I don't know what dying looks like

MICK. I need help

LISA. and so I phone the GP

it was about two in the morning   and so the GP wasn't there   I was put through to the emergency GP and he was absolutely cruel to me   he said, 'I'm not coming out   there is nothing I can do   and if you need any help, get him to the Homerton Hospital   I'm not prepared to come over'

'but he's in real pain   he's really ill'

'he may be in real pain, he may be very ill, but if he's that bad, you take him to the Homerton   yes, ring an ambulance, and get him to the Homerton'

Mick was screaming at me from on the bed

MICK. I am not dying in the Homerton   I am not dying in the Homerton

LISA. don't worry, Mick   I won't take you   I won't take you

he lies down and then it was agony and he sits up and he is shouting and unbelievably I was so exhausted I went to sleep   I lay down and fell asleep

and that was just a terrible night

the morning came and he was still conscious

and as I left Mary came   I'm going back to work today, get some stuff done and then I'm coming back

MARY. I felt that we had been deserted

Thirty-Three

DIANA *and* GEORGE.

DIANA. but then there was   how do we get him up, back to his bed?   he was clearly too weak to be got back upstairs   so then I decided, right, that here was the moment and next door to the sitting room on the first floor was a little bedroom with a little kitchen   so I thought, well, I'll put him in that bed for the night, and then I'll get the hospital bed ordered   it was a Sunday so I couldn't do it that day   and I rang up, and the hospital bed came the next day and, apart from getting up to do the last concert for charity, he didn't really get out of bed again   he'd get up to use his commode   so, that's not quite true, that he didn't get out of bed   once the dementia was bad he'd struggle to get out of bed

he stopped eating

I'm beginning to feel incredibly tired, but I am busy   not even making one-egg omelettes any more   ice cream, he could still eat but somehow there's a lot to do because the hospital bed was fine   he liked being in the sitting room because he was surrounded by his collection of paintings, and he had two bedside tables, one on one side of the bed, and one on the other – because there had to be identical objects on each side of the bed   so, if he woke up facing one way, he couldn't always turn over easily in bed to get what he needed   and by the bed had to be a glass with five cigarettes in it – no more, no less   there had to be five   there had to be three lighters on each side of the bed in case he dropped them   there had to be his glasses   there

had to be a glass for his water   an ashtray, certainly, if not
two   oh, yes   there had to be three ashtrays on each side
of the bed because, once he'd put the cigarette stubs out in
an ashtray, he wants another ashtray to put on top, so he
wouldn't have the smell of the stubs   then he'd put some
more stubs in that one, and there'd be another one put on the
top   everything was becoming very, very – demented –
because it had to be total order, and he had to be keeping
control of his two bedside tables, and they had to look alike
in some way. So, if he woke up facing one way, it was the
same as if he woke up facing the other way   I quite
enjoyed it

now I was sleeping in the little room next door, with the two
doors open   and I had a baby alarm so I could hear him
when he turned over

Thirty-Four

DAN *and* NELL.

NELL. this is what happened

At six thirty on Sunday morning, after getting up to go to the
toilet, Dan called me to help him back to bed   soon he
became uncomfortable and was having difficulty with his
breathing   his lungs were bubbling and he felt he was
drowning   he asked me to get help and, as instructed, I rang
the district nurse's night number

a district nurse and a student nurse arrived at six fifty-four
a.m.   she decided he needed morphine and went to set up
the driver   she found there was no morphine in the box and
therefore no point in setting up the driver   she managed to
get him to swallow one green and one purple MST tablet,
with a little water

she said her shift was finishing and she would pass him on to
the day staff   and they both left

Dan was now experiencing extreme discomfort, and he asked me to get help   I rang the hospice that had been visiting Dan for about two years, and was told there was no one there who could speak to me, and to ring back after eight thirty a.m.

at about nine a.m., being still alone and Dan suffering, I rang the hospice again, and spoke to the same person   I said I needed help urgently   I was transferred to an answer machine   I gave up

I put a little Oramorph in Dan's mouth, but it ran out   I gave him Lorazepam, but that came out too

at about ten a.m. a daytime district nurse arrived, and again searched the box for morphine   she left, and came back with yet another district nurse   they crowded into the bedroom and discussed the situation with extreme anxiety

they rang an out-of-hours doctor to come and write a prescription for morphine

Dan asked me to get help for pain in his chest

at about eleven a.m. a doctor on call arrived and asked the nurses what strength of morphine they wanted   they didn't know and he became irritated and cross with them   he spent a long time looking in his book and arguing with them

Dan tried to ask the doctor for help but by this time he couldn't speak clearly   but the doctor didn't examine or even look at Dan – not even casting a look in his direction, let alone a gentle reassuring word

Dan tried to get out of bed, but I lifted his legs back in and he lay down again   he was agitated and struggling to stay calm   I know him so well   he wanted a dignified death

after consulting a book for some time, the doctor wrote out a prescription   there was a lot of talk about which chemist might be open on a Sunday   nobody knew   the doctor was annoyed about how to find morphine and suggested various places   then he left as he went, I said, 'thank you for coming'

'don't worry, I get very well paid for this,' was his reply

the nurses left, to look for morphine

Thirty-Five

TRICIA *and* PHILIP.

TRICIA. a few weeks before Philip died he decided he wanted to go to Greece – to the mountains that he loved and where he had painted and so we went off to Greece, with a letter from the Home Office giving us permission to take all his morphine: a case full of drugs

we stayed in a little flat, but I could see the tumour on his liver growing bigger every day   but I was practical   he wanted to paint, and I went swimming and I could see him loving every minute of it – painting among the olives

I know everybody has to die but I was in control of the medication and I have that knowledge   and I knew how to calibrate the drugs, and I was there all the time   I could tell when he needed more or less of each drug   I could tune in   he had one that lasted twenty-four hours and then, if he had a breakthrough pain, I could give him a combination of drugs   I got into the knack of doing that   he was the most unneurotic person   he wasn't preoccupied with any of that

I think the thing that helped was that I had knowledge   I knew about pain control and drugs and medication   and I wasn't afraid of people dying in my arms   I really minded about death being dignified and people not having pain, because nowadays people shouldn't have to suffer either physical or emotional pain   pain is so debilitating, so destructive

Philip's and my philosophy was: life is short and you might as well make it good while it lasts   and it was good   and Philip was always more interested in what he was reading or painting or designing to get too worried about things

we came back from Greece exactly two weeks before he died   on the way out I'd arranged a wheelchair, but on the way home he walked   when we got back to Heathrow he walked

Thirty-Six

DIANA *and* GEORGE.

DIANA. but then he has one or two fainting fits   and I'm getting help from the district nurses and I get a care package

– they gave me twenty-one hours a week, because George's job had become, by this time, almost non-existent   I think he had about one gig a month, which he was taken to   but otherwise he was just in bed, and not left alone either, because of those fainting fits

a woman called Mary came and she'd give him a bath – a blanket bath   and then she'd come in the evening so I could go out and do some shopping, or something   and then the district nurses would come

every time they came they wrote in a notebook what they'd done, and they used to leave it here for the next nurse to see   and they would come about two or three times a week, and a palliative nurse came   next to prognosis they had written, 'short'   and that gave me a turn

and by this time the district nurse had brought me the package of all the medication   she'd brought a thing called a syringe driver with her   and there were three lots of medicines that we had, which could be put into it   we had morphine   we had a thing if you had too much phlegm – but

that made his mouth dry, so that was awkward to give
him   and then there was a Valium-type thing, in case he got
agitated – because, she explained to me, that sometimes, just
before somebody dies, they can get very agitated not
necessarily, but that can happen

I don't think we used the morphine more than once or twice,
at the very, very end   but the first time we put the syringe
driver in, we put it in his thigh, and he just immediately
pulled it out   so then we put it behind his left shoulder,
where he couldn't reach it   and we were still managing to
talk quite a lot – not a great deal, but we managed to tell him
a couple of jokes, which he liked   and he told me a joke –
such a quiet little voice, I could hardly hear it – but I was
always pretending to laugh at his jokes anyway, so I just
laughed   and there were lots of people coming to see him

and I had always thought there was one girlfriend that I
would never allow in the house, but he really wanted to see
her   so she came and I remember my heart was
thumping   that was her day for coming

thumping and thumping

and, actually, it was fine   when somebody is dying an awful
lot of rubbish goes out of the window   and sometimes two
or three people would come in a day   and some people were
very, very good, and just sort of quiet   it was wonderful to
just sort of sit there… women, on the whole, make better
visitors

Thirty-Seven

TREVOR *and* LESLEY.

LESLEY. she wanted me to wash her body   she was very keen
on being clean, and she didn't want to smell, or her breath to
smell   she said, 'please wash me   you don't think me silly,
do you?'

'oh no, Mum,' and I washed her all over   it was very important for her to be clean   she wasn't a vain person   I don't want you to think that   but she wanted her dignity every day, a clean nightie

I needed someone at night   I may have been a bit frightened of being on my own with her   I thought if I could get a good night's sleep, I could cope so we got the Marie Curie nursing team in   these are nurses who give up their time to sit with terminally ill patients   wonderful angels – who would stay awake all night, so she had company

Mum was happy with that, though she was getting weaker and didn't always know what was going on

Thirty-Eight

MICK, LISA *and* MARY.

MARY. but then a doctor came and two specialist nurses and they gave him morphine   I instantly felt they know what they are doing and they had a lovely gentle manner and they were just so gentle   two black women   they appeared to me to be very highly trained

Mick was getting weaker and drowsier, but I think he heard and knew what was going on

he definitely knows we are there, me and Jessica   and the nurses tended him so beautifully

The day he died – (*Cries and then is angry.*) the kitten is running around   really, there was so much rushing around that day   Mick deciding to die at home definitely placed a huge burden because there were so many arrangements to sort out

Mick seemed to be getting kind of weak and drowsy   but he had the television on all the time   he was obsessed with films   he had TCM showing all the time

MICK. That day   I think it was the day I died, *Rio Grande*, my favourite was playing

Sound of a cowboy film.

MARY. me and Jessica – we just held his hand, one each – and he just slipped away

LISA. Mary phoned me

MARY. 'Mick's gone'

LISA. 'what do you mean?'

MARY. 'he's dead   he's dead'

LISA. and she screamed at me

MARY. 'he's dead'

Thirty-Nine

DIANA *and* GEORGE.

DIANA. now, he really isn't eating anything, and he isn't drinking   he's even stopped smoking

GEORGE. when I first stopped smoking, I stopped smoking for about a week, and then, 'I think I want a cigarette'

DIANA. 'no, George   don't you remember, you've given up   you have nicotine patches now'

GEORGE. 'oh, yes   I forgot'

DIANA. I'd stopped being bad-tempered, and yes, I did like looking after him   sometimes I slept on the sitting-room floor, on a rolled-up mattress, because sometimes he would wake and struggle to get out of bed   and I remember once I was downstairs with some women friends, and we were having a game of cards   and I said, 'I think I'll just pop up and see if he's okay'   and he had managed to swing his legs

over the rail on the bed, and he didn't know what he was
doing or quite where he was   and all three women came up
and we all tried to get him into the bed, and we just
couldn't   we just couldn't get him back in, somehow   and
he was really agitated by this time   and I rang the district
nurse   and half an hour later a district nurse came round,
and she managed to get him back into bed   but on the whole
he was peaceful   so, the last five nights I had a Marie Curie
nurse   I went to bed in the room next door, and she sat in
here with him   and they don't sleep   they just stay awake

Forty

TREVOR *and* LESLEY.

LESLEY. Trevor was now on the scene   he came and sat with
her I might cry when I tell you this

the thing I couldn't come to terms with was watching her
die   this was a huge thing for me   I was terrified – terrified
of the process   it was as if this was all about me in some
way   I felt guilty about that   it is Mum who is
dying   Trevor asked her if she was frightened   and she
said, 'no I am not frightened   I have never been frightened
of anything'

I said, 'Mum, I'm going to miss you   how am I going to
live without you?   and she said, 'I want to be with your
dad'

I was frightened, but I wanted to be there

she was on a morphine driver by this stage because she had
started to hold herself and feel uncomfortable around her
bottom area   at this stage she wasn't talking, or eating   I
was giving her sponges to suck, and the nurses gave her a
catheter

I walked into the bedroom and something didn't smell
right   Trevor was downstairs and when I lifted up her sheet
– she was wearing pyjama tops but no bottoms – and I could
see she was bleeding from her bottom   she was semi-
conscious, and she put her hand round and felt the blood, and
she was aware she was bleeding

I rang the nurse but she couldn't come back for a while, and
she told me what to do: 'roll her over, move the pad and put
another one there, and roll her back'

I couldn't do it on my own, so Trevor and my daughter,
Laura, had to help   she was naked from the waist
down   and I remember, as we were doing it, I felt it wasn't
right – Trevor seeing her, and Laura seeing her grandmother
naked – and she wouldn't like that   it made me very sad

TREVOR. Mum had blood on her hands   there was blood
coming out of her and she had touched her bottom, and
Lesley and I cleaned her up she was like a child   I saw her
as a young girl   her face had changed   she was very brave

  I held her, while Lesley cleaned her

LESLEY. we did it as quickly as we could

Forty-One

DAN *and* NELL.

NELL. I was alone with Dan   I lay beside him and talked to
him   his breathing was very rapid   he was opening his eyes
and looking around   he echoed my words of love, but he
could barely talk

it was good that he was in our double bed because I could be
beside him, and talk to him   his eyes would open and search
for me

I am here!

he seemed to go in and out of sleep

I am here!

Primrose got on the bed and lay alongside him

after about two hours, his breathing went quiet, and he seemed to be sleeping peacefully   he opened his eyes for a moment and he looked at me in a blaze full-on   I kissed his hands and lay close to him

then he shut his eyes and I think I dozed... on and off... keeping him company   after about twenty minutes, he stopped breathing

I think he died at about one thirty in the afternoon

at about four o'clock the nurse returned with the morphine

she had been searching for it for five hours

Forty-Two

TRICIA *and* PHILIP.

TRICIA. as a nurse I had spent a lot of time with people who were dying and I got really miserable when there was any kind of deception going on, either between the doctors and the patients or between the patient and their relatives, because the one thing that is so important, when you're at that point in your life, is the truth   the truth is more important than anything   then you can trust – which you can't if the people you love the most are all pretending

when Philip was ill I always went with him to the hospital, and when they told him there was no hope – the cancer had spread to his liver and to his bones – he said, 'I don't mind about dying,' because what we really believed in was being

together and then things were good, and you loved every day
because you loved each other   and it was good while you
were alive

he said, 'I don't mind about dying, and I know that we're not
going to see each other anywhere else, so the only thing I
mind about is parting from you'   and he said that to all four
children as well

there was no taboo about dying, and perhaps that set the scene
in our house   everybody talked about it, and didn't pretend

Forty-Three

DIANA *and* GEORGE.

DIANA. each night I started to say goodbye   every night I
said, 'this is goodbye   it's goodbye'

GEORGE. 'goodbye!'

DIANA. but then there he would be, still alive the next morning.

and then a friend said to me, 'well, have you told him it's all
right for him to die?'

and I said, 'no, I didn't know I had to do that'

so I said to George that night, 'you did your will, and the
children have been to see you – they've all been and
everything is okay   all your plans are as you wanted them
and, you know, you can let go' and he would look pleased
yes, he would look pleased about it

then, the next morning, there he was!

it was a different person every night and they all wrote in the
notebook   and sometimes they were a bit frightened of the
two yappy little dogs that I had

there was one very nice one, Mary, an Irishwoman who liked dogs   she was there the last night and she wrote in the notebook: 'Diana and I changed the bed'   and George looked up at her and smiled, and whispered, 'goodnight'

and then I went to bed

she wrote, 'at twenty past two I called Diana as instructed, because his breathing was changing, and she came in and she sat and held his hand, and then, after a while, he died'

and I kept that page. I tore it out   and I've still got that bit of paper

relief   tearful relief   you know – at last

Forty-Four

TREVOR *and* LESLEY.

LESLEY. once the morphine had kicked in, she didn't seem to be in pain

TREVOR. the night she died I was sitting downstairs, watching TV   and the TV suddenly stopped   it was broken   I went upstairs and I said, 'oh, I loved that TV and now it's died' and Mum laughed   she had a huge sense of humour

she was so weak she couldn't speak but she laughed

soon she seemed to be asleep, and Lesley said, 'why don't you go to the pub?'   and I did

LESLEY. I walked into the bedroom, and she was making this difficult breathing noise, and I was crying, and I said, 'Mum, you have to go, it's time'   and I shouted at the top of my voice, 'you have to go! it's time!'

I think she heard me and I started counting her breaths: one, two, three   and then she'd do another huge breath   I was

kneeling and holding her hand, and I shouted again,
'Mum   you have to go!'   and she took a great breath, and
she opened her eyes   and then, there was nothing   and I
held her hand and sobbed

then, I felt euphoric   it was such a privilege, such an honour
to have been there   and I put a red rose in her hand   it was
the most wonderful experience of my life, and it was just us
two that felt right – that Trevor wasn't there   it was just
us   I had been there from the beginning, from the day she
was admitted to hospital   I had been by her side to the end

I'll never forget those district nurses   they were my closest
and dearest friends, and I'll never see them again

TREVOR. I'd just ordered a drink and my phone went, and it
was Lesley saying Mum had died

LESLEY. for Mum to die the way she did was the best she
could ever have hoped for   quietly, in not too much pain, in
her own home, with her daughter and her son nearby

Forty-Five

MICK, LISA *and* MARY.

LISA. we stayed together all day   Mick was lying dead on the
bed, and Mary and I, and Jessica, and my other sister…

Jessica cooked a meal   and it was just a small flat, and we
waited with Mary for the undertaker who was coming

MARY. and the undertaker came   Mick wore his Armani
suit   the one he bought in Rome

they wrapped him in one of these new linen sheets, and took
him away

I just went to sleep in the bed where he died   and the next
day I changed the sheets

LISA. I came back the next day and Mary and I spent the day together   I took the day off work   and we sat around the table together   and we just stayed together   and the cat moaned, and cried, and was very upset

MARY. Mick wanted to die at home

MICK. and I did

Sound of a cowboy film.

MARY. I kind of regretted I didn't spend more time with him that last week (*Cries*.)   I'm sorry I went on going to work   I thought I should

Forty-Six

TRICIA *and* PHILIP.

TRICIA. Philip adored his food, and Pip came into the bedroom first thing that morning and said, 'Dad, I'm going to make you some porridge for breakfast'   and he cooked this porridge, and I had fed him a few mouthfuls, and he had eaten it

and then we'd all got on to the bed, and Philip put his arms around me, and he just died

all five of us were on the bed with him, and my sons are very tall   the moment he died, we were all there together   we were all there perhaps we all knew he was going to die that day   from the day he was diagnosed till the day he died was exactly six months

and I think that is one of the things about cancer: it is a very unviolent death, especially if the symptoms are controlled

I'd been with a lot of patients who died, and I think my philosophy is that life is so precious; that you don't have

guilt, and you don't have regrets   you live well, and you
live well with the people you love   and then you die   we
were married for thirty years, and we had six months to
grieve together – to share the grief   I feel really sorry for
families where the death had been sudden   no time

Forty-Seven

DAN *and* NELL.

NELL. in all, five National Health staff attended Dan's death:
two night district nurses, two day district nurses, and one
out-of-hours doctor   yet not one was trained to help a dying
man   and none of them offered human support

after Dan died, all his children came, and my sister came,
and my children came   and we lay on the bed beside him,
and cried and talked till late into the night and Primrose lay
alongside him and never moved till the undertakers came
and took him away

he died at home, where he wanted to be

'this has been the happiest year of my life,' he had said a few
days ago

we had got so close

'what will I do without you?' I asked

'I don't know,' he said

'what will I do without you?'

I don't know   I don't know   I don't know

The End.